My deep, dark, evil, twisted & fucked up mind.

Joshua P. Johnson

Copyright © 2023 Joshua P. MacNeil-Johnson

All rights reserved.

ISBN: 9798852916747

This book is dedicated to a few individuals.

It is dedicated to my brother Justice,

When all hope was lost to me, he told me "Pursue the art".

It is dedicated to Danielle,

The first person I spoke to about making this book, who looked me in the eye and said, "do it."

It is dedicated to every single person who took the time to open it. To anyone who reads any word on any page and feels anything. To anyone who's ever questioned themselves, their life or their choices.

There are no rules here,

Punctuation, style, format and subtext are out the window. Things will rhyme when I want them to, or they won't. Maybe it's just words, maybe it's a song. I'm not even sure I know at this point.

What I know is that I am no trained writer, yet had stories to tell, experiences to share, and emotions to be rid of. So that's what I did, and I hope you enjoy it. If you don't that's okay too, move on and have an excellent day. But if you stick around, you will be looking into my heart & soul.

The things I filled this book with are the way I carry on. Written to help exercise my own demons and process what I am feeling. Based on true stories or real emotions. It talks of thoughts of suicide, sex, substance use and loneliness. If you wish to proceed knowing that, I thank you.

CONTENTS

Part 1:

My mind.   1

Part 2:

How I'm fixing it.   71

ACKNOWLEDGMENTS

I would like to take a moment to acknowledge the kind support of my friends. Health care workers, students, young professionals, musicians, lovers, writers.

Without their support, this book would not have come to fruition.

I thank Noah, Carrie, Tyler, Tosh, Brandon, Emily & Nate.

My best friends.

part 1

My mind.

Goodbye,

Don't call,

I hate you,

You disgust me,

I will never forgive you,

How could you,

You were better than this,

I loved you.

Things I wish you'd said before you left.

Joshua P. Johnson

Knock knock.

Who's there?

It's your intrusive thoughts.

My intrusive thoughts who?

It's me, I am you, here to self-sabotage all that you do.
All that you are,
All you could be,
I am here to destroy it, it's just you and me.

No one is home, and you might as well leave.

Well, it won't be that easy to get rid of me.
I'm awake when you're sleeping, I run while you walk.
I throw out the subtext whenever you talk.
I will not go anywhere, it isn't allowed.
I will not be leaving; you will have no ninth cloud.

My deep, dark, evil, twisted & fucked up mind

A crisis in your head is a party to the right mind,

Add anxiety to pain, by love you must divide,

Take the answer that you have, your happiness you will subtract,

Multiply your lack of faith, then square root all your troubled facts,

Despite how you react to this, your answer equals all your strife,

Look yourself hard in the mirror,

try not to take your own life.

Joshua P. Johnson

You blink until the image clears,

You wash away the crust and look deeply into your own eyes,

Your pain so blatant in this reflection,

You splash the water on your face and bury the emotions deep within,

Your image now stoic and proud.

One last glimpse at yourself before this day begins,

One last thought,

Pathetic.

My deep, dark, evil, twisted & fucked up mind

Every scan of my brain,

I hope to see something wrong.

A sign to show me that it's not who I am, but something I've become.

Looking for something to show me that this isn't all my fault,

Yet every scan has me healthy.

Right as rain.

Good to go.

A picture of perfect health.

If I'm so God damn healthy, then why do I feel this way?

Why do I see a monster in the mirror every single day?

Joshua P. Johnson

A love story, Chapter 1

While I do not know her all that well,

Her attitude and views seem all to swell,

Her skin seems still so young and soft,

With laughter that would get you lost.

4 years with braces bleeding her cheeks,

The rest of her life with her beautiful teeth,

20 years of walking on this earth,

A lonely soul who gives wide berth.

This isn't true love, but it's a tricky spot,

Since I feel better when she's here than I do when she's not,

A five-year difference has some take and some give,

With so much of her youth still left to live.

Yet I wonder if I'm in her mind as often as she is in mine,

And if she sees through the charade when I say that I'm fine,

She comes round my soul and asks if I'm good,

If I could better hide that I'm not, I would.

You can take my freedom,

Take my soul,

Take my friends, my family.

You can stand up and block my path.

Stop everything good that has come my way.

I will kill you.

Things I say to the mirror every day.

"You mistake me for someone who cares about what you have to say."

Is what I say to your face while I panic inside.

Don't let the truth get in the way of a good story,
Even if that story's yours…

Chug back the story telling through paper straws,
Tell a joke to break the ice and wait while it thaws,

You're the reason for your failure but you are not the cause,

Embrace your flaws, break all the laws, nearer the moment draws,

Act self-deprecating, then pause for applause.

Fog,

A mist that blocks the sight of my past, a vast disgrace,

Impeding vision of a time and place, that is mine.

Seeking out the young man I have erased,

Searching for the faith that I've misplaced,

Haunted by the life that now lies in waste,

Moving on at a zombie's pace,

Dissect my mind, try to crack the case.

Case closed.

What a fucking waste.

My deep, dark, evil, twisted & fucked up mind

Notice of intent:

Open your eyes, as the daylight breaks through,

It will not get easier despite what you do,

Despite what you've done, from your life you must run,

Or contemplate deeply with the next loaded gun.

So, christen yourself anything but savior,

And live down the shame of all your poor sick behavior,

You've done all your time,

Been sentenced for crime,

Yet will not get better even if you rhyme.

You're bouncing ideas all through your brain, but try not to focus so much on the pain.

Why won't you get better? Or deal with your strife?

Truth is it's worse when old friends are twisting the knife.

Some friends have left you, others have not. Old friends have stated they'd like you to rot.

Your family's still here, if not disappointed,

From messiah to demon, you are freshly anointed.

So, move right through,

Take them with a grain of salt.

You won't sleep tonight,

Your career's at a halt.

It looks like it's over,

The end of your world,

And what's it all over, you've screwed over a girl.

Yes, you did do it, brought this on with your actions,

But sadness begets you, from this reaction.

My deep, dark, evil, twisted & fucked up mind

Dear Diary,

   Today I finally

                                             but I still hurt.

Joshua P. Johnson

What is a soul?

The space between body & inner mind?

A place where your inner beauty *lies*?

The debate seems meaningless,

As they will all go away in time.

Yet each time I seem to catch a glimpse I remember,

I've already sold mine.

My deep, dark, evil, twisted & fucked up mind

My eyelids close,
But not for the last time.

Well maybe,

Ask me in the morning.

Joshua P. Johnson

Day by day we live our lives, every single sunrise.

All your relative success is failure through the wrong eyes.

Your shoulder to cry on, betrays you when the moment dies,

Just another bad influence who's otherwise occupied.

Hypnotized each day, by beauty in the daylight skies,

Then lose the optimistic hope each day when my soul cries.

Each day that I awake and open up my freshened eyes,

Is another day I dread, my downfall's what my eye spied.

peacefully last night in my sleep, underneath the glooming sky

peacefully last night in my sleep, is how I wish I'd died.

My deep, dark, evil, twisted & fucked up mind

I'd hate to be MAD.

Take aim at her love,

Find solace in her smile.

Feel a wash of happiness, for just a little while.

Make love to her soul, then put that love on trial,

Another broken heart, another crooked smile.

In time you will move past her,

Move past this whole affair,

In time you will stop loving her,

Since her love was never there.

How is it that someone can be surrounded by those that they love, yet feel true loneliness?

This is a mystery I would like to solve.

However, I am no detective.

You are not your worst memory, nor are you your worst action.

Joshua P. Johnson

Little boy you are cursed with my DNA,
Destined to suffer through all of my darkest days,
I'm disappointing those who surround themselves with me.

Run before you catch my agony,
I will stay because there is no hope for me,
Say goodbye to our friends and our family,
All in time.

You don't know me the way that you think you do,
I will only destroy and then abandon you,

So leave me behind and move on with the things in your life.

Let me see my life flash before me,
Let me die for the sake of our family,
let you run, get ahead of our misery.

Start some music, turn this poem to a sad song,
Start it over, don't cry, sing along,

I'm amplified by your love, but you don't know me at all.

Every day will not always be Sunny,
Every song won't be a beautiful Melody,
Thank mother Teresa for the gifts she has given me,
Seek Justice for my lack of empathy.

These words are my soul, and it doesn't have long.

Just throw me out before I waste away,
This family can't go on like this every day,

End it now, the ancestry dies today.

My deep, dark, evil, twisted & fucked up mind

A love story: next chapter

It has turned out I didn't know her that well,

One day it's great, the next day is hell.

Every moment by my side was a moment of joy,

It took a harsh truth to see I was only a toy.

Not sure how to justify the way that I feel,

I was in love, but her love was not real.

Every moment I run, I sneak, and I hide.

Add it to the list, reasons for my suicide.

You can call it dramatic, call it a fluke,

But when I think of her now, I just want to puke.

I want to cry; I want to scream, and I want to die.

I want to fight, I want to get angry, I want to make this a war, but I just want so much not to be sad anymore.

I want to not feel the way that I do.

But if she got to read this, my death is on you.

Joshua P. Johnson

Although I'm surprised by solemn reactions,

I can live with the sins of my actions,

Can you?

My deep, dark, evil, twisted & fucked up mind

One more drop in the bucket is enough to make it overflow,
Yet one drop doesn't fill it at all.

This is the battle in my mind.

To be too much,
Yet not enough.

To be all right,
Yet still be wrong.

Expectations we are supposed to exceed,

<u>Yet cannot meet</u>.

Joshua P. Johnson

Momma I'm sorry,
I must put up a fuss,

This game that I play is not fair to us.

Momma I'm sorry,
I'm not who I wanted to be,

But I am not proud, I've disappointed me.

I know that you love me, know I love you. But it's hard to get behind the things that *you* do. The things that you don't, the things that you won't. I start to question my thoughts, when I think of our home.

I'm not asking for more,
Or mad we were poor,

I just need to say I can't pretend anymore.

Our lives are not healthy,
We must do better,
I will go first and be the trend setter.

I thought that you'd take this, as a personal attack,
So, I kept these words to myself, since I did not want that.

Now here we both are.

Cruel & Ironic,

What a time to live on planet earth.

Alone

Can something be lost, if it was never found?
Would I ever be missed, if I wasn't around?

Could the world that we live in ever come to a stop?
I'd feel better if it was, that I would if it's not.

This existence I'm in feels like my mind has gone mad,
How can I ever move on, if I'm truly that bad?

I guess I'm really that lame, that pathetic and absurd,
But if I could only pick one, then *alone* is that word.

Harlequin: a person who amuses others by ridiculous behavior.
Synonyms: Buffoon, clown, goofball.

Once upon a time,
There was a damaged boy,
Who had mastered all the arts, of turning pain to joy.

When manipulating pain, and twisting it to fit,
The boy had quickly found,
The joy made was not his.

He crafted it for others,
They laugh and cheer for him,
But when he stops and thinks about it, torment is what it gives.

Painting on his smiles,
To try and fix his frowns,
Telling detailed tales & hymns of times his life turned upside down.

Gathering reactions, a clown is what hes become,
Getting rises out of folks,
To laughter he succumbs.

He may not like it now,
But this is all he's got.

He'd like to become something else,
And hopes with every thought.

It's cold.

The rain pours,

The wind picks up and the grey skies come,

Thunder claps,

Lighting strikes,

The storm rages on.

The sun comes out.

My deep, dark, evil, twisted & fucked up mind

Dear God,

A lot of people ask me lately, how I've been doing.

A lot of people want to tell me, things that I should be doing, or how it is I should be feeling.

I tell them all it's okay, but in reality,

I'm weak in the knees.

-

Weak from the souls of my feet,

until my soul feels defeat,

until the one last time that my heart has to beat.

I'll keep on walking the streets,

bonding with the strangers I meet,

building up my fucking mind till it can't fathom defeat.

So this fucking fake sweet Judas better prepare to repeat his defeat,

Bent over doggy style while I fuck him, this bitch is in heat,

Bake him like a pie, then reheat and serve him up like raw meat,

This Judas in my mind better retreat, before I chew him up and excrete.

Joshua P. Johnson

But I'm fucking myself and my dicks concrete,

look him in the mirror, throw some insults and repeat,

then leave him in the past, you're the elite,

or return your soul to G, O, D and hope he kept the receipt.

So take a load off and celebrate to this,

Rub a genie make a wish,

Your cult will draw you another fish,

They got lots of sins for you to fix.

Or would if you gave a shit,

So fuck you, pack your bags and split,

Then submit to my wit, because I spit trash talk, or at least I moan a bitch.

I said dear god, but I wonder if you're really kind,

Because Judas killed your son and now you let him kill my fucking mind,

Is this the life you designed, or am I self-confined in my own mind, self-undermined while I lack the strength to rewind how I've been unkind, fucking those I've enshrined, then exiled by my own kind,

So, God I may of fucked myself, but bitch you co-signed.

Fade to black.

Your story is over.

Exit stage left.

Hold for applause.

Silence.

Curtain call?

Read the news, wear my shoes, walk a mile then drink some booze.

Smoke some weed, barely sleep, wake up, leave, forget to eat.

Embrace pet peeves, heart on your sleeve, dodging questions, duck and weave.

Now you know.

I deserve sympathy, I deserve help.
I put that cigarette back up to my mouth,
Although I know life doesn't owe me shit,
I don't want to be in it.

I just want them to like me,
I just want it to be likely,
To amount to anything and know this isn't it.

Not to spend another night alone and know my life is shit.

Joshua P. Johnson

Just looking for a little growth,

To prove I'm not just a piece of shit.

Or blow my brains out soon enough and never discover it.

Going through the motions every single fucking day,

Celibate & sober, still feel disgusting in every way.

Lose your life, lose your friends, lose your job and lose your wife.

Fuck them all and fuck you too, you've lost in life and that's the truth.

Just give up, stop even trying, look in the mirror and stop fucking crying.

Press a gun against your brain, pull the trigger to end your pain.

End your passion, end your hate, save those around you, this is your fate.

You're nothing now, your life is blank.

Emotions bare, an empty tank.

An empty shell of what was once a man,

Or just,

A boy.

The way a sad song can change your state of mind,

Why is it such a simple thing can cause such a reaction?

If we had the answer, we wouldn't be any better off. But we might just be a little less curious.

Joshua P. Johnson

I remember the first time I hurt you.

I remember promising never to do it again.

I don't remember lying.

But here we are.

My deep, dark, evil, twisted & fucked up mind

I'm stewing in my bad thoughts 24/7
Taking all these bad thoughts all the way to heaven,

Click clack, lock back and cock that gun, pull the barrel
from your brain and go and have some fun.

Fuck that, wake up, open up your eyes,
just another bad dream from dark and gloomy skies.

Bad thoughts with me every single second,
Intrusive thoughts that follow me 24/7.

Call me OJ in the courtroom, charming with no evidence,
Can't talk about my feeling since you're lacking in the relevance.

No one really gives a shit and I'm absent in their presence,
my lack of presence will be a present, my presence is what they won't miss.

So ill drink to that, eat that or pop that pill,
Hoping every single time this is the one that kills.

Joshua P. Johnson

Just keep going.

If to exist in society is why we are grown,
Why am I so alone?

If I'm so God damn alone,
How do I create a home?

I will walk the road, the coop has been flown, I will destroy the status quo and exist on my own.

Counting down the days,
Until my life changes forever.

Counting down the days,
Until they all see I'm not clever.

Counting down the days,
Until I leave for my endeavor.

Counting down the day,
Until my friends all leave together.

Process of comparison

Love is a marionette,
It is hard to maneuver,
And it comes with strings attached.

A marionette is a puppet,
Its purpose is to be manipulated,
It has no control.

A puppet is a façade,
It gives false perceptions for your joy,
Because it is not real.

Joshua P. Johnson

I'm daydreaming of your face,
Of a time and place where you could be mine,
Or would be. If that's what you wanted.

Second place in your race,
but could be winning in mine,
Or would be. If that's what I wanted.

I Sleep deep while my dreams of you repeat,
Without you, I feel incomplete,
No longer able to be discreet,
It's time to admit defeat,

And move on again.

So smile bright white because things aren't really all that bad,
Just because you lust for something, doesn't mean it's yours to have.

My deep, dark, evil, twisted & fucked up mind

My love has become lethal,

All the people I have hurt have been some loving people,

I'm on fire,

I need to stop drop and roll,

Leave a path of burning bridges everywhere I go,

But there's fire,

Burning in my heart,

Writing rhymes and processing for perspective in my art,

So stand clear,

H2O is here,

An extinguisher is trying to put me out, but I'll remain right here.

On fire.

Joshua P. Johnson

Looking for a diagnosis,

Call it lactose intolerance,

I'm all out of honour and

I'm as peaceful as Swiss,

But not making the Cheddar,

I can't make my life better,

A mental bed wetter.

Because I'm scared of my dreams,

You might call it cheesy,

It's so redundant to me,

I no longer want to love Bri.

So, I'm blue like the cheese,

I'm begging you please,

Help me up off my knees,

I'm not admitting defeat.

My deep, dark, evil, twisted & fucked up mind

I'm a mental grilled cheese,

My minds halloumi to me,

Don't melt if you turn up the heat,

So back to writing these beats.

Not tart and soft,

But got myself by the throat,

So forget what you know,

And then bow down to the GOAT.

Joshua P. Johnson

I rarely smoked dope,

I never did cope,

Had help from close friends, but I said nope.

From life I did run,

My good I did shun,

I could have been just, but this was more fun.

I let my life rot,

Then I smoked pot,

I killed my old self; it was an onslaught.

My deep, dark, evil, twisted & fucked up mind

Sleepless nights,

Filled with frights,

Down to the nubs my nails I bite,

Waking days,

In a haze,

Lighting drugs up in a blaze,

Going home,

To write a poem,

Through my mind and brain, I roam.

The cost of finding the people you love is living your life without them beforehand.

My deep, dark, evil, twisted & fucked up mind

You roll your young body out of bed,

And ignore the creaks and cracks,

You sit up and endure the pain, in your knees and in your back.

2 cigarettes and some ibuprofens are your tasty meal,

Hoping someday you will feel better, and your injuries will heal.

You have a stretch and start to wonder if it's your T's or L's,

Peculiar pain all up your spine has your body in a hell.

Plus, there's your knees, that they say are fine,

You're young and they will heal.

But don't forget the carpal tunnel.

The burning eyes,

The clicking wrist,

Or your big flat feet.

Tylenol when you get home, but at least you are alive,

There should be no pain to feel, since you're only twenty-five.

Joshua P. Johnson

Rain keeps falling on the street,

Sounding out for my echolocation,

I've been lost for quite some time,

Wondering why my mind has been on vacation,

The darkest of all my thoughts have been deep in gestation,

Sitting in on Satan's reservation,

A full blow dissociation.

Rain keeps falling on the street,

But the smell is my aberration,

It ceases my aggravation,

It is my liberation,

My only salvation.

2 truths and a lie

I'm in love with the way I feel in my own skin.

The love I hold for her is never wavering.

I see hope for a better tomorrow.

Sit down with a stranger as they pick apart your life.

They delve into your business, and they dive into your strife.

Taking cliff notes of your memories,
Guidance you ought to know,

But your heart is so cold.
It doesn't rain, it snows.

St. Jude,

Give me strength, because I am just so tired.

Sincerely yours,

A lost soul.

For fucks sake.

Why?

Why did you say those things to me?

Why couldn't you mean them?

Why did you insist on saying that you did?

Conversations half spoken, once haunted my mind.

Locked in my own brain, by the laws of time I am not confined.

We're afraid to confront, feelings intertwined.

To all our love, all others are blind.

But we have chosen this, it was not assigned,

In the race for your affection, others are falling behind.

Joshua P. Johnson

You were the heaviest of rains,
While I was the moss.

Absorbing every drop that I can,
Not an ounce to go to waste.

You were the brightest of suns,
While I was the plants.

Taking in your rays,
Energizing myself with you.

You were a gift to my soul,
A band aid on my wounds,
Fresh air in my lungs.

You are still here,
But I am rotting.
Rotten.
Dead inside.

Freaking out,

Hiding now,

So all the people here don't get to see the show,

A dancing monkey with a tale they already know.

Stare at the sea,

I can't have the things god hasn't granted me,

With no more hope,

But lots of shame and misery.

Joshua P. Johnson

> Take all that I have,
>
> I have given all I can.

I wish I could love you,
The way you want me to.

Sparkling diamonds, with a hint of blue,
Finding beauty in your eyes, when mine is all through,

There is so much left,
But what should I do,
But share my kindest thoughts with you.

Your skin is white, but cheeks are pink,
Make a stupid joke, then we share a wink.

Laugh it off, cry inside,
So embarred that we could die,

You & I.

Trying my best to keep my autonomy,
And stop practicing these bad roles,

But don't practice sodomy, because people shouldn't be fucking assholes.

Yet here we are, our morals are bending,
We might get to cum, but there's no happy ending.

I'm stuck in this loop,
I'm all out of hope,

Don't know what to do,
Tie a long length of rope.

Hang it from the ceiling,
Because she's out to get me,

Yet I did this to myself.

I'm done, no longer in control,

Salvation is too high on the shelf.
I cannot reach it all by myself.

Body found by someone else.

Joshua P. Johnson

The best part of my life is that it's ending,
Because I don't think I can do this anymore.

I'm tired of drifting on and just pretending,
I can't keep my guard up anymore.

So, I hold my breath,
And count to ten,
And hope for a day that never comes.

Life

Build up your life,
Like I'm building this poem.

You search for yourself,
You seek, and you roam.

Trying to build,
On what came before,

Adding new content,
Not closing the door,

Keeping it open,
To let new stuff in.

Playing life's game,
Trying to win.

Approaching the climax,
Where a prize should await.

But in the end, it falls flat.
How disappointing.

I spoke to God today,
To see if this is just a scam,

His vision soon disappeared,
Time to chew another gram,

Have a glass of red wine,
Make another tea,

Have another vision,
See what I will see.

I'll speak to the devil,
While looking in the mirror,

Blink away hallucinations,
See myself much clearer.

I hope I can cope,
Like soap on a rope,

Bend me over backwards, while I take the scope.

Take a good look inside me, to see what you can find,

I've found nothing good yet, and I look all the time.

It's happening now,
Yet I'm haunted by my past,
Seeking my independence as she's slipping from my grasp.

Call it desperation,
Could be my ADHD,
She may be running through my mind, but she's driving me crazy.

Why does my mind get so attached,
Deep emotions I must dispatch.

No hope for my future if I can't let go,

I must learn to be on my own,

This I know.

The love is gone,
The bond, the grit, the passion.

How long will I hold on?

Left, right, left.
A pattern I've known for nine long years.
But no more.

A comradery that forgot me the day I left.
But I will remember forever. I think.

I hope not.

Friends I will remember, good times that will be with me forever.

But the system that left me behind deserves to be forgotten.

Joshua P. Johnson

It's been, a longer road to Nova Scotia than I thought,
I started smoking pot and taking mushrooms.

I've been, dreaming of a day where I don't reap what I ought,
Where I don't cry myself to sleep in my own bedroom.

I can, find myself some friends,
Where I'm not just a mean to their ends.
Who don't throw me to the side for all my mistakes.

I'm done waiting for that day,
It was here yesterday,
All you must do is turn to the next page.

Part 2

How I'm fixing it.

Caterpillar

I'm not quite happy, but don't know this feeling.

I'm standing up tall, the old me is kneeling.

So, I'm on my way.

The "up & up"

Just plain fine.

I could be all better, in due time.

So, let me be.

To heal my brain,

To stew in my memories and process my pain.

For I would like to change into someone else.

Yet still, be me.

There comes a time in each person's life when you discover who you are,

When the moment comes you will often discover you were not who you thought.

The person you promised you would be was not even close,

They were so far,

You slow down and come to terms with the fact that you were a complete piece of shit,

Your persona gets a face lift,

Your wrists, some brand-new bracelets.

"The truth will set you free" is said so often,

Yet it's the truth that locked you up. Justifiably?

The guilt of your actions is a little lighter,

The ability to repent and absolve seems almost a possibility.

You just have to *try*.

Life can seem so cruel,

With no hope to be found,

Stuck in your daily routine,

Spinning round and round,

The days may seem so dark,

You're not stuck, its just a rut,

So just stay the course my friend,

Because the sun is coming up.

Matthew 7:2

"For the same way you judge others, you will be judged. With the measure you use, it will be measured to you."

Today I learned the bible tells a true story.

When the hand twisting the knife belongs to those you once called friend, the pain is tenfold,

This is the reality I have brought on myself,

Not much left to lose,

Not much left to say,

Those left here beside me fight harder every day.

My deep, dark, evil, twisted & fucked up mind

I've all but given up,

I've put this onto others, their pain I can never know,

Except my pain is bringing shame and fear more than you ever could know.

I was faking smiles before,

I thought I had it down,

Now I must hang my head in shame when gallivanting around.

So what is left to do, but write my sins away,

And hope I wake tomorrow,

Because *tomorrow is a brand-new day*.

Jessica

A brief moment in time in which you wonder if the love is real,
The same moment in your day in which you contemplate the world,

Taking every single moment that you share for granted,
Contemplating in your head, your friendship on this planet

You genuinely love her so much you can't stomach all the feelings,
Appreciate all her love and having trouble breathing.

Accepting her quirks and finding joy in all the things that make her weird, embrace this solemn kinship that you've always feared.

Look into her eyes, that sparkle like a city and contemplate how you've earned the friendship of a soul this pure & pretty.

A slow breath in,
A slow breath out,
A million years pass in just a moment.

A slow breath in,
A slow breath out,
Every problem just fades away.

A slow breath in,
A slow breath out,
Feel peace for once in your life.

Butt it out and put it in the ashtray.

Everything comes rushing back all at once and you wonder if it's even worth it.

It is.

Joshua P. Johnson

A love story, final chapter

I put my hate on you,

It was not fair to do,

My self-doubt and fear were crystal clear, But not to me and you.

I fell into love,

Then fell into hate,

To protect myself from hurt and pain I gave you the blame.

I was not well,

I still am not,

It was with myself that I should have fought.

I got too attached,

From all of my own issues,

you showed me compassion, compassion that I misused.

You've moved on now,

Or I hope you have,

We no longer speak, but that's not so bad.

My deep, dark, evil, twisted & fucked up mind

I no longer dream of you,

I no longer think of you,

You are in the back of my mind.

I still call you friend.

I still appreciate the time we shared. The love we made, or the Pokémon we caught together.

But for you I no longer yearn, and I never really should have.

And I'm sorry.

Joshua P. Johnson

Dominion street and skinned knees,

Corner stores and memories.

I split my lip when I took my bike off the porch, this is who I am.

Poetry and bad dreams,

Playing games and watching TV.

8 stitches when I fell from a tree, this is who I am.

Decent grades and then the army,

I am strong and you will all see.

Build myself credibility, this is who I am.

Find a girl who loved me.

Build a life that's happy,

Then burn it all to the ground, this is not who I am.

The first step in personal growth is understanding.

Understanding that sometimes you won't be enough.

Understanding that sometimes you will be too much.

Understanding that the people you hurt aren't ever forgiving you.

That you caused hurt to others, and you can only do what you can do, for you.

The second step is acknowledging.

Acknowledging that your actions have permanent consequences.

Acknowledging they may never trust anyone again, not just you.

Acknowledging that the effect you have on others can be permanent,

That you caused hurt to others, and you can only do what you can do, for you.

The third step is accepting.

Accepting that you can only be better than who you are today, tomorrow.

Accepting that they may not care,

Accepting that you must live with the consequences of your actions,

That you caused hurt to others, and you can only do what you can do, for you.

There is simply No Way

Some people are like you,

And some people aren't.

However, some people are, and they aren't.

A person that can be so like you, yet so different.

How can this be, well I would think there is No Way,

However, this No Way is here, every single day.

The evidence is apparent, No Way has become my best friend.

No Way has been here since I found them, and I'd like them to be here until the end.

The No Way defies reason, or judgment and neglect.

The No Way has peculiar reasons in the way that they perspect.

I knight No Way my counselor, to help me through my crimes,

The true transparency of No Way has helped me through my times.

The possibilities are endless.

Each timeline in view,

Every option there for something new.

wade through, review, pursue the taboo, let it stew, your mind askew, this is new for you, find evil to undue, a full-on coup, think of what to do, the good ideas and pick one or two, your answer is due, but you don't have a clue.

Try again,

Start anew.

The answers *will* come to you.

My deep, dark, evil, twisted & fucked up mind

Danielle

Christen her so stunning,

Her pale skin and her gile.

Christen her a close friend,

And hope she stays a while.

Christen her the kindest,

With freedom in her smile,

Christen her a good friend,

With love that is inferred.

Christen her your kin folk,

No lust behind the words.

Christen her a confidant,

Although it sounds absurd.

Christen her this poem,

I wrote it just for her.

Christen her this farewell, the writing is almost through,

Christen her her-own description since this describes you.

Joshua P. Johnson

You have clawed you way deep into my mind,

You are not what I was trying to find.

When all that I feel is death and decay,

I can look into your eyes, and you will take my breath away.

So, climb your way up out of my brain,

Take with you all of my desires,

Take with you all my pain.

I've started my life over anew,

I find myself still dreaming of you,

And then I watch you fade away.

I wish you'd fade away.

Pacifier

When my mind wanders, there is a place that takes me to the start,

A dark and gruesome past that is hyperbolized in art.

The written trope once helped me cope,

With feeling lost and lengths of rope,

The time is now to focus on the present, to find something to make my mind pleasant.

Someone nice to pacify my thoughts, or maybe share them when they are feeling lost,

There's someone here,

existing in my life how it is, a peculiar friendship with a wunderkind.

A solemn soul with much I share, a pale young human with long brown hair.

A fresh young mind, that's as lost as mine, and still tries to hide it all the time.

That's okay, its who we are. Artistic minds looking from afar.

So, we stand right in the thick of it, moving forward, wanting to quit.

But it's not in us, although it's all we feel, day by day, a turning wheel.

Others don't see it, but you don't need them,

We are moving forward,

This is not the end.

FIN.

My deep, dark, evil, twisted & fucked up mind

I sat across from you,

Silent.

Unable to communicate in your presence.

But I learned to speak.

Breath taken every moment you sat there,

A bead of sweat on my brow.

It took a minute,

But I learned to speak.

I learned how to see,

How to hear,

How to find you when you got lost.

But first, I learned to speak.

Like a child on the floor,

Unable to make a sound,

Through practice,

I learned to speak.

Joshua P. Johnson

When the day is warm,
You forget until a cool breeze sweeps through,

When you hate your job,
You acclimate until you find something you like to do,

When life is unfair,
You struggle until you find those that are there for you,

Don't get complacent.

My deep, dark, evil, twisted & fucked up mind

You may share their blood,

You may have served together.

DNA may bond you forever.

You may have shared a cell,

Or both braved frigid weathers.

The point is, you've gone through hell together.

You may not share a father,

But may share a mother,

The point is you're there for one another.

Through thick & thin, clean & dirty

This is the context of my brothers.

Joshua P. Johnson

Walking there so slowly,

A snail is what I've become,

Wishing each and every day for a life where I could run.

Taking in each sunset,

And basking in the rain,

Hoping for another life with love instead of pain.

Opening with daybreak,

And finishing with night,

I only yearn for a single day in which I would not have to fight.

So, break your status quo, Rise to the occasion, grow.

Bring about this change yourself.

Yours comes from you,

Mine comes from me,

It comes from no one else.

My deep, dark, evil, twisted & fucked up mind

Less than a lover,

yet more than a friend.

I'd have held on tighter,

If I knew this was the end.

Don't be so hard on yourself,

Don't be so mean,

Your nightmares won't end,

When you're living your dreams.

Check in with your emotions,

Don't have so much fear,

If you think you are happy,

It's downhill from here.

These words hold no meaning,

They tell no more truths,

If they're going to mean something,

It's *all up to you.*

Joshua P. Johnson

I will be okay.

Well, maybe I will,

Maybe I won't be.

Maybe I'll get lost wading through society.

Maybe I'll swim, and come up for air,

Maybe I'll sink and get trapped down there.

Maybe I'll drown, or get lost to the town,

Maybe I'll make a smile out of my frown.

Maybe I'll climb my way up from this hell,

There's no way to know,

But time will tell.

My deep, dark, evil, twisted & fucked up mind

A beautiful melody that rings through the air,

A pass time singing joy is what he does bare,

Blending the days, singing our praise,

Telling us stories until the end of days.

He won't run from the street ghosts,

Singing old folklore tropes,

Fixing our hearts,

Just trying to find us a little hope.

Joshua P. Johnson

Fall nights,
On the couch,
Sipping on red wine.

Blue dye,
Your soul cries,
It's interwind with mine.

Fake plants, and real ones,
New clippings from the vine.

A stage, a spotlight & a crowd.
Keep you going all the time.

So, mic check,
One two, one two,
You might play music for us,
But you play your soul out for you.

My deep, dark, evil, twisted & fucked up mind

I used to call myself selfless,

Screwed and lied, and now I'm helpless.

Look in my eyes, don't know who this is,

Make a change, I will get through this.

Write some more, rhyme through my mindscape,

You get one life, there is no escape.

So work on yourself, get all the help,

Find some good friends, you will always have wealth.

Now I am rich, no money to spend,

I am rich in love, wealthy in good friends.

Joshua P. Johnson

While I can look in the mirror,
And see sparkling blue.

It does not compare to the beauty of you,
A wonderful brown, with a beautiful hue

Theres's beauty in eyesight, between me and you.

The shape of the clouds,
Can be all that I knew,

The sky in the sunset,
With orange and blue.

The sounds of the harbour,
Are giving me hope,

So, I am still climbing,
Not at the end of my rope.

Because all that I know,
Is I seldom do cope,

Pessimism in daylight,
In darkness there's hope.

So, I battle my own mind,
On this slippery slope,

Then sit on the shoreline,
And wonder if I'll float.

Joshua P. Johnson

The scent of my cigarette smoke mixes with her perfume,

Mixed until we are one.

The lotion on her skin leaves her smooth to the touch.

And I do, touch.

Write line after line,
About ending my life,
Ink from my pen,
Blood from my knife.

A mind left in darkness,
Is all that I know,
But the day that I died,
Was a long time ago.

I am someone else now,
I do not know who,
Ill explore me,
You can explore you.

Seek some self-growth,
Expand your closed mind,
A small patch of empathy,
Is what you may find.

Grow compassion for others,
Walk a mile in their shoes,
You light the match.
I'll light the fuse.

Dad,

It's been a long road,
Although it doesn't seem so.

Dissecting lots of lies and truths to craft the man I know.

The past, it does not matter,
I don't even know it all,

Focusing on what came before could lead to our downfall.

I haven't said this to you,
I should have screamed it out so loud,
But no matter what you've ever thought,
Your story makes me proud.

Of the man you are, or were, or could be.

Of the things you've said to guide me.

The judgments you have passed on me.
Or lack thereof.

My deep, dark, evil, twisted & fucked up mind

END.

Authors note:

In the end, this book was released months after I had originally intended. I could not find it in myself to say "it is finished" no matter how many poems I added, or how much editing I did. While I could not figure out what was wrong with it, I knew in my mind that it was not yet complete.

In my heart I knew what I wanted from it. I wanted to look at this book and feel like it represented who I am, on the deepest level. The problem faced is that each day we change as people, slowly but surely. One day an acquaintance said to me "do you even know who you are?". When I concluded that I did not, I knew maybe it was time to swallow my pride and realize that that my goal was not achievable.

With that being said, I hope that I came as close as I could to my original goal. If you are reading this, it means you took a good long look through my heart and soul and then stuck around to the end.

Thank you.

Sneak peek at:

"Like & Subscribe"

Joshua P. Johnson's next poetry collection. A fairly neutral satire designed to bring attention to the world as we know it. Exploring subjects such as use of social media, sex & porn, finances, political controversy, and the general state of the world.

Release date to be determined.

A nursery Rhyme.

I wake up in the morning and scroll on the gram,
Big brother can see, wherever I am.

Going to the slaughter they lead this little lamb,
But they make us lead ourselves because they know that they can.

So pat-a-cake, pat-a-cake bakers' man,
Hypnotize me as fast as you can,
Like me, follow, share me with your friends,
Im building up my profile to prepare me for the end.

Because I'm a little teapot, short and stout,
They've got us by our handle,
Their drama we spout,
And when we got all steamed up,
Hear us shout,
Big brother is watching, but we are devout.

So Jack and Jill go up the hill,
But Jack can't go any farther,
The world hates him, he cannot win,
Jack will die a martyr.

So little pig, little pig let me in,
Our agenda has ways to hypnotize your kin,
So like us, love us, let us have your kids,
Or little pig, little pig we will blow you in.

Step 1. Separate you from your kin.
Step 2. Let our schools take them in.
Step 3. Teach them how it ought to be.
But they won't learn it from you, because they're learning from me.

Your family has no value, your old school genetics,
are very inconvenient since you are spreading strong ethics.

So, you should have more children, like an old school catholic,
Build up a young workforce to vote for our cabinet.

Ignore our agenda, go back to social media,
Keep in-fighting and ignoring what we're feeding ya.

Joshua P. Johnson

True Fans.

Little boy,

Do you want a girlfriend?

It only cost four ninety-nine.

You can pretend you have her love,
One month at a time.

Type away at your love letters,
Get all the pictures that you want.

She's spending all your money,
But it's her you get to flaunt.

Once your month has finished,
And maybe so did you,

You can always subscribe again,
I bet she wants you to.

Printed in Poland
by Amazon Fulfillment
Poland Sp. z o.o., Wrocław